Wholesome Classrooms:

*Keeping ♥**Heart**♥
at the Heart of Every Classroom*

by

Sonya R. Johnson

Preface	5
Introduction	8
Wholesome	14
Hard Work	21
Optimism	28
Leadership	36
Educate	45
Service	52
Order	57
Mentor	66
Enjoy	73
Wholesome Classrooms	79
Parent and Faculty Emergency Phone List	82
My "TO DO" List	83
Journal Writing	84
Suggested Readings	92
Acknowledgments	93

About the Author...**96**

Preface

*Wholesome Classrooms: Keeping **Heart** at the Heart of Every Classroom* is written as a handy partner to help you succeed in the classroom and throughout your teaching career. It is meant to be easy to read and enlightening at the same time. It is not designed to be an intellectual stimulant, just simple, practical guidance for teachers in diverse and even in at-risk schools.

I want to help new teachers fall in love with teaching. I personally know that love is the unconditional and unwavering component that will fuel your voyage in this profession. It's important that new teachers protect the institution of education by educating the whole child. All children want to be successful and it's your job as a teacher to help them become successful at something. Not every student will obtain straight A's, but all students come to us with knowledge, be it good or bad. Our profession requires that we cultivate, harvest, and extend that knowledge. The fact is, what we do in our seasons of educating children transcends the actual time spent in the classroom with us. Children almost always remember the good, the bad, and the ugly that make up their school days. In which category will your students view their days in *your* classroom?

As educators, we must make every effort to impact them positively. It's especially crucial at this time in America to effectively equip our children cognitively, emotionally, and socially. As teachers, we help build the paths and roads that lead our children to become better doctors, scientists, professionals, citizens, and human beings. Children today need quality education from quality individuals working in a quality environment. Make sure that you are that teacher!

Introduction

Wholesome classrooms are learning environments that are beneficial to the student's social, emotional, and cognitive development. Wholesome teachers are imperative for the integrity of a student's educational experience.

For many students, teachers are the gauges that set the thermostat favorably or unfavorably in a child's academic quest. This is an awesome privilege that we as educators have inevitably received. It's time to produce teachers in this millennium who will successfully exhibit and execute wholesome values, genuine concern, and scholastic competence in the classroom. New teachers who really want to get a strong anchoring in the classroom will benefit from reading these pages, while experienced teachers who want to rekindle their passion for this profession should keep reading, as well.

I'm sure we can agree that new teachers entering classrooms today are vastly different from their counterparts of thirty years ago. Those teachers who started many years ago had the assistance of strong adults, hardworking parents and grandparents, and involved communities who saw to it that children had a village of support. Thirty years ago, children were taught at home that school was important—they knew that disrespecting a teacher was not an option. Parents made it clear to their children that 1) they were to be quiet and pay attention in class, 2) they were to attend class short of death, and 3) they were to obey the teacher above all else. All children, regardless of their IQ or ability, understood that teachers' opinions and advice were highly regarded. Being a teacher thirty years ago was a symbol of status and achievement, especially in minority communities. Many saw teaching as a calling for people who possessed an instinct woven with wisdom and maturity.

Today, it's very different. Many young teachers have not experienced the impact of village rearing, and many lack the instincts of our predecessors. Today's teachers are faced with all kinds of opposition from parents and students, and the profession is not as well-regarded and esteemed as it used to be. **This is why it is more important than ever to know who you are and why you teach!**

In spite of this, as a teacher you do have some advantages. You have a network of teachers, administrators, professors, researchers, and community leaders at your fingertips.

Learn from the network of professionals around you. Professionalism is a "must-have." Professionalism encompasses expectations, conduct, dress, communication, and work ethic. Wholesome classrooms begin with wholesome teachers.

As educators we are responsible for children's destinies, therefore we must be certain that we are living our own destinies as educators. You must know, *in your heart*, that you would rather teach more than anything else. Teaching cannot be a second or third choice of career because your first choice didn't work out. It's hard to be happy with a second choice. "I am going to be a good teacher," "I am going to make a difference," or "I have been called to be a teacher" are nice things to say, almost clichés, but do we really understand the responsibility behind those statements? It grieves me to see that we are approaching an era in education in which the *heart* in teaching is dwindling. Although contributing factors may be significant, the overall consequences are crippling to our children. Your success is not dependent on the state of the economy or what community your school is in. You were not meant to exist in a mediocre classroom. You *can* build a Wholesome Classroom!

In reading this book, be prepared to enter into another dimension of a teacher's responsibility, to gain another perspective of the teacher's role in a student's destiny, and to get a renewed awareness of the importance of developing a wholesome classroom. You do not need to be hindered by the limited perceptions of others or the lack of resources that our profession can entail. Discover time-tested techniques and principles that will enable you to fulfill your purpose in the classroom, no matter where you teach. This handbook is designed to encourage novice teachers (and experienced teachers, too!) so that they may fulfill their dream, discover their purpose, and find themselves building a Wholesome Classroom.

Wholesome

Definition:[1]:

1. promoting or conducive to good health or well-being; healthful
2. tending to improve the mind or character
3. characterized by health and vigor of mind and body
4. tending to suggest health, or soundness

Synonyms:

nutritious, nutritive, nourishing, beneficial

Wholesome Quotes:

He who loveth a book will never want a faithful friend, a wholesome counselor, a cheerful companion, or an effectual comforter.

Isaac Barrow

The world is upheld by the veracity of good: they make the earth wholesome.

---

[1] All definitions and synonyms are taken from Dictionary.com Unabridged (v 1.1), based on the Random House Unabridged Dictionary, © Random House, Inc. 2006, and The American Heritage® Dictionary of the English Language, Fourth Edition Copyright © 2006 by Houghton Mifflin Company.

Ralph Waldo Emerson

The whole art of teaching is the only art of awakening the natural curiosity of young minds for the purpose of satisfying it afterwards; and curiosity itself can be vivid and wholesome only in proportion as the mind is contented and happy.

Anatole France

A good and wholesome thing is a little harmless fun in this world; it tones a body up and keeps him human and prevents him from souring.

Mark Twain

In the course of my life, I have often had to eat my words, and I must confess that I have always found it a wholesome diet.

Winston Churchill

Periods of wholesome laziness, after days of energetic effort, will wonderfully tone up the mind and body.

Grenville Kleiser

A 'good for you' feeling that's evident due to attitudes and practices for a well-rounded experience.

SRJ

W is for Wholesome

One thing I've tried to provide for my students is a

wholesome classroom environment. I started with a name: I called my third grade students "Johnson's Jewels." They knew without a shadow of doubt that they were special because they were jewels. My motto was, "Where precious gems are cultivated into exquisite jewels." Many had a hard time adjusting to fourth grade because they wanted to remain jewels. I would have to remind them regularly that I still loved them and that they would always be jewels, but that they had to move on. It did my heart good to see them cherish that time with me. Many would come back years later just to say, "Hello, I'm doing fine." They would, of course, mention that they missed being in third grade!

- ♥ Building a hearty, healthy classroom and curriculum are essential elements in the classroom.

- ♥ Set high expectations for your classroom as it relates to behavior, homework, rituals and routines, conflict resolution, etc.

- ♥ Only allow words and actions in your classroom that are positive and beneficial for the whole group. Students must understand from day one that only nice words, good work habits, and pleasant gestures are allowed in your room and in your presence. Anything contrary is banned from your classroom. Be sure you honor and model these same characteristics in front of your students. No matter how hard things get, "grin and bear it" because you can!

- ♥ Set age-appropriate consequences when expectations aren't met. Be consistent when apportioning rewards and consequences. Children need consistency. The rules in my classroom were simply to respect everybody in the school (teachers, other students, and yourself) and to be accountable (work habits, making choices). They were challenged to be self-reliant by being responsible for the tools needed for daily productivity, by learning the content and components of the classroom, and by taking the "golden rule" approach to problem-solving and conflict resolution.

- ♥ A word to the wise: be sure that your overall communication and execution of your expectations—especially as they relate to rewards and consequences—are compassionate, sincere, and firm. Students must feel like a person, not a number. And remember that the classroom is not the place for prejudice. Maslow's hierarchy of needs stresses the importance of "belonging": your students must believe that they belong in your class and that it's not an accident that they are there, because you have so much to offer them. Once that is established, then they will trust you to take them anywhere on their educational journey. All your students must see you as fair, available, and approachable in that classroom, regardless of race, socio-economic class, or ability. If you are partial to a particular group of people, then seek employment where those people are. You will not be happy or effective in this profession if you are not working where you want to work. Your classroom must be a positive and risk-free learning zone.

♥ Wholesome classrooms are rooted in mutual respect and quality instruction. Put-downs, teasing, fighting, or disrespectful behavior should not be condoned in your classroom by anyone, at anytime. Building a risk-free environment is crucial to facilitating a wholesome social and learning atmosphere in your classroom. Your personal philosophy should include tenets such as, "All children have good in them" and "All children can learn." Your students can sense if you are genuine or not.

Reflections

In your opinion, what is a wholesome classroom?

_____

_____

_____

What are some practices that you can institute in your classroom that will help you to cultivate a wholesome environment socially and cognitively for your students?

_____

_____

_____

Tips for a Wholesome Classroom Environment:

- Develop an age-appropriate physical and learning environment.
- Set high expectations.
- Praise often.
- Instruct using varied techniques and strategies.
- Practice skills.
- Evaluate.
- Remediate as the evaluation dictates.
- These tips work for behavior modification, general climate control, academic instruction, and mainstreaming.

Hard Work

Definition:

1. exertion or effort directed to produce or accomplish something; labor
2. productive or operative activity
3. the result of exertion, labor, or activity; a deed or performance

Synonyms:

apply oneself, be gainfully employed, buckle down, carry on, dig, do a job, do business, drive,
art, calling, career, craft, employment, job, line, métier, occupation, profession, pursuit, trade, vocation, endeavor, duty, hustle, labor

Hard Work Quotes:

For every disciplined effort there is a multiple reward.
Jim Rohn

Don't judge each day by the harvest you reap, but by the seeds you plant.
Robert Louis Stevenson

Do not wait; the time will never be 'just right.' Start where you stand, and work with whatever tools you may have at your command, and better tools will be found as you go along.

Napoleon Hill

I want to be thoroughly used up when I die, for the harder I work the more I live. I rejoice in life for its own sake.

George Bernard Shaw

Purposeful and focused actions geared toward the success of a specific goal or lifestyle.

SRJ

H is for Hard Work

Experience has taught me, as well as others, this fact: creating a wholesome classroom is hard work. Developing a wholesome classroom just doesn't come about in the time between the open and the close of a school day. Hard work involves learning the strengths and weaknesses of every personality in your class, and building a learning environment that will enhance each strength and strengthen each weakness. Much of a teacher's preparation is done while the children are gone. One of the saddest sights to see, in my opinion, is a new teacher leaving ten minutes after the children have gone for the day, with empty hands and an unconcerned air. Teachers must put time into their craft, especially in the honeymoon years. You must put time and effort into planning meetings, workshops, staff development, and book studies, in order to enhance wholesome instruction. Your administrator will be more apt to keep you around if he or she can see a drive and a desire to do well. Never shy away from ideas or new programs that can enhance you professionally.

Hard work also encompasses practical and proven discipline strategies that will require consistency and active enforcement. Another sad thing to witness is watching new teachers try to correct behavior "at will" in spontaneous intervals, without valid corrective procedures. Just like instruction, discipline must be systematic and consistent. Believe it or not, you will burn out faster by being lazy in this profession: putting forth the effort to institute procedures and routines in the first few weeks of the school year will deliver greater results than by trying to address issues as they arise. Wholesome classrooms require hard work to create and execute an effective curriculum, seasoned with preparation, and mental and physical stamina.

Reflections

What's your general philosophy about work?

_____

_____

_____

What areas of concern do you have as you reflect upon the magnitude of your responsibilities?

_____

_____

_____

Tips for Making Hard Work Trouble-Free:

- ♥ Never be afraid to ask for help.
- ♥ Keep and file away everything from your first few years of teaching (for example, important documents, certificates, etc.).
- ♥ Keep your school calendar, work assignments, and substitute list nearby. Be sure to program your principal's, secretary's, and team members' numbers into your cell phone. You never know when you will need them.
- ♥ Keep a photo library of all your bulletin boards, learning centers, science projects, etc., for the first few years.
- ♥ Ask for copies of assignments or lesson plans that teachers have found to be successful.
- ♥ Utilize Internet resources.

- ♥ Get to know your parents and devise ways to utilize them in or for your classroom.

- ♥ Dress properly so that you can work properly. Look like a leader! Too tight, too short, too sheer, or too revealing clothing are for after school hours. Cover up your piercings and your tattoos—many students find them distracting. Watch the messages you send even when you are not talking. After all, it's not about you—it's about the children. Mature people understand that.

Optimism

Definition:

1. disposition or tendency to look on the more favorable side of events or conditions and to expect the most favorable outcome
2. the belief that good ultimately predominates over evil in the world
3. the belief that goodness pervades reality
4. the doctrine that the existing world is the best of all possible worlds

Synonyms:

anticipation, assurance, brightness, buoyancy, calmness, certainty, cheer, cheerfulness, confidence, easiness, elation, encouragement

Optimism Quotes:

I have had dreams and I have had nightmares, but I have conquered my nightmares because of my dreams.
Dr. Jonas Salk

If they can make penicillin out of moldy bread, they can sure make something out of you.
Muhammad Ali

I try to avoid looking forward or backward, and try to keep looking upward.
Charlotte Bronte

An optimist is the human personification of spring.
Susan J. Bissonette

Optimism refuses to believe that the road ends without options.
Robert Schuller

Optimism is the faith that leads to achievement; nothing can be done without hope.
Helen Keller

I will have what I say, pursue, and expect, no matter what comes my way. I will be triumphant in my endeavors.
SRJ

O is for Optimism

Never allow the negative occurrences of the day before to dictate the days, weeks, months, and years that follow. There are times when the day before may include an unfortunate experience with an irate parent, an unsupportive administrator, or an uncontrollable child. Learn the "Art of Forgiveness" quickly. Remember to leave each day in the past, or else you will become bitter and lose your spark. Expect each day to be great and benefit from that self-fulfilling prophecy. Try hard to embrace and hold onto only the good that each day brings and quickly discard the bad. Take a daily dose of honest optimism! Allow your personal philosophy to include expectations that favor the best possible outcomes each and every day. Don't allow the flaws of our profession to become a fatal opponent in your quest to cultivate a wholesome classroom.

Teach the "Art of Forgiveness" to your students as well. This is a great tool for solving petty arguments in class. I taught my students to forgive each other from day one. They must be taught to let things go. Also, teach your students to expect the best in life, no matter what side of the tracks they're from. Each day I would have my students read aloud daily affirmations and inspirational poems. I discovered that they can learn to read the poem *Hey Black Child* by Eugene Perkins just as quickly as they could learn *The Three Little Pigs*. By teaching them that poem, I teach them about good character and self-esteem; I give them a poem recitation that they can perform on any stage, especially those last minute programs we teachers have to prepare for; and I have a prompt from which to instruct them in writing skills.

There are many poems that have inspirational meaning and that can serve several purposes in the classroom. The words will come back to them in the years to come, even when they least expect it. Also, it's a way to input good thoughts that can possibly be transformed into good actions. In other words, we have a hard job, but we cannot lose hope, we have to stay positive, and we have to get creative!

Reflections

What are the good things that will happen in your classroom today and everyday?

_____

_____

_____

I promise to trash the negative today because if don't then...

_____

_____

_____

Tips to Keep Me from Falling Off the Optimism Bandwagon

- ♥ Recite a positive affirmation as often as needed.
- ♥ Eat a Hershey's Kiss.
- ♥ Dwell on the good things for thirty seconds.
- ♥ Sing or play a happy song in class.
- ♥ Celebrate a student's success, no matter how small.
- ♥ Read a joke to the class.
- ♥ Read the obituary section of the newspaper to yourself (at least you're not in there!).
- ♥ Freeze the class and DEAR (Drop Everything and Read).
- ♥ Fast forward to arts and crafts time.
- ♥ Vent <u>once</u> to a trusted "vent partner." This person should be one who will not judge you for feeling badly. Choose someone who can say something to help you get back up

and try again. Remember, venting for the sake of venting is complaining, and that's counter-productive to building a wholesome classroom.

- ♥ Create your own diversions: when things get tough I will . . . .

Leadership

Definition:

1. the position or function of a leader
2. the ability to lead
3. an act or instance of leading; guidance; direction
4. the leaders of a group

Synonyms:

command, direction, lead, management, authority, domination, guidance,
hegemony, helm, initiative, skill, supremacy

Leadership Quotes:

The task of the leader is to get his people from where they are to where they have not been.
Henry Kissinger

The task of leadership is not to put greatness into people, but to elicit it, for the greatness is there already.
John Buchan

You do not lead by hitting people over the head—that's assault, not leadership.
Dwight D. Eisenhower

Leadership is not magnetic personality, that can just as well be a glib tongue. It is not "making friends and influencing people," that is flattery. Leadership is lifting a person's vision to higher sights, the raising of a person's performance to a higher standard, the building of a personality beyond its normal limitations.

Peter F. Drucker

The true leader serves. Serves people. Serves their best interests, and in doing so will not always be popular, may not always impress. But because true leaders are motivated more by loving concern than a desire for personal glory, they are willing to pay the price.

Eugene Habecker

Equipping, guiding, directing, and coaching lives positively and effectively.

SRJ

L is for Leadership

As teachers we serve as leaders for our schools, communities, churches, and households. As leaders, we are instrumental in building highly qualified schools, wholesome communities, better churches, functional adults, and civilized cities. We have a tough job, but don't forget:

tough jobs are doable. It was a tough job for Columbus and his crew to organize a voyage to the New World; it was a tough job to lead uneducated slaves to the North; it was a tough job to get a black man elected to the office of President of the United States; but it was done! Many have done tough jobs before. As teachers all we have to have is the knowledge to teach the content, the personality to inspire and touch every person in that classroom, and the current research that helps us to make the right choices for instruction. We have to take these ingredients and connect them to the power source within our children and empower them to grow and progress.

Educators like Booker T. Washington and George Washington Carver are proof positive of the success that enriched the past. Local and state "Teacher of the Year" rosters are testimonials to a teacher's ability to affect the world. Let's face it: teaching is not a career for stoic, callous, perverted, or insensitive people. As teachers you will find yourself needing skills on multiple levels, such as public relations, problem-solving, conflict resolution, and Motivation 101.

It seems we've entered an era when schools are forced to require background checks, install metal detectors, hire police, and limit extracurricular activities just to protect everybody. Even in elementary schools there is a need for officers on occasion and, for proactive measures, there is a need for resource officers. (In schools where this resource is available, these officers should not be a component of your daily classroom discipline plan.)

I've heard teachers, especially new teachers, say, "I'm

teaching everyday—it's up to them to get it." Many teachers are taking a "hands-off" approach in a profession in which many students need a "hands-on" experience facilitated by courageous, well-trained, and well-rounded leaders. I often watch the big blockbuster movies that spotlight teachers who, against all odds, made a difference in the lives of their students. I've found that it was the common denominator called courage that helped them to make that difference. Super teachers are not one in a million—we can find super teachers in every school district. As a new teacher, please seek them out and learn from them.

As a leader, people see you before they hear you. Fellow teachers, parents, and administrators will size you up at first glance. Building a wholesome classroom involves you looking like the adult and acting like the adult in that classroom. We must be careful to look the part, act the part, and live the part, especially around our students. Pet peeves should not govern your classroom. Teacher's pets should not be the management plan for your classroom. Teachers should never date students (unfortunately, a growing phenomenon with new high school teachers).

Be the leader in your classroom: model and facilitate effective practices that can easily be mirrored by your students. Some fads and trends in fashion are not appropriate in the classroom. Teachers in low socio-economic communities must dress the extra mile—you may be the first professional your students will see. Drop the runway look (micro miniskirts, low rider blue jeans, spandex, visible thongs, and peek-a-boo blouses), drop the hip-hop craze, and please put up your tattoos. Look like the professionals we're grooming our students to become. Respect is hard enough to achieve, but it's even harder when the teacher is on the level of the students. Mature people can handle this reality.

Reflections

What is your general definition of an effective leader?

_____

_____

_____

What attributes do you as a teacher possess and should possess to be an effective leader?

_____

_____

_____

Tips to Make You a Better Leader

- Remember the teachers who impressed you the most. What made them special? Now employ those aspects in your career.

- Study the lives and contributions of effective teachers and leaders of the past and present.

- Listen to the children around you. What are the things they desire in a teacher? What are the things they hate about teachers? Take heed!

- Keep a look out for the "go-getter" in your school. Listen, look, and learn.

- If you could pick your child's teacher, what would she or he be like? Is that you?

- Stay prepared, stay flexible, and keep your expectations for yourself and your students high!

Educate

Definition:

1. to develop the faculties and powers of (a person) by teaching, instruction, or schooling
2. to qualify by instruction or training for a particular calling, practice
3. to provide schooling or training for; send to school
4. to develop or train
5. to inform

Synonyms:

coach, discipline, instruct, school, teach, train, tutor, acquaint, advise, apprise, enlighten, notify

Education Quotes:

Organize, agitate, educate, must be our war cry.
Susan B. Anthony

Those who educate children well are more to be honored than they who produce them; for these only gave them life, those the art of living well.
Aristotle

The object of education is to prepare the young to educate themselves throughout their lives.

Robert M. Hutchins

To educate a man in mind and not in morals is to educate a menace to society.
Theodore Roosevelt

Raising competence cognitively, morally, and emotionally, with functionality.
SRJ

E is for Educate

Educate every student in your classroom, no matter his or her IQ. All children can learn something. Utilize technology, peer coaching, individualized instruction, small groups, learning centers, children's literature, experiments, field trips, videos, songs, poems, community fellowships and programs, and the like. Leave no stone unturned when teaching. Use visual, textual, kinesthetic, and auditory stimuli. Model and teach moral character traits, good manners, and sportsmanship. Use humor from time to time.

Educate the total child, socially and academically.

The majority of lessons taught are not found in a textbook. Be open! Find the "go-getter" in your school and then adopt and adapt the techniques and strategies that work for him or her. Become very familiar with your state's curriculum recommendations. A wholesome classroom foundation is built upon the efforts and effectiveness of quality instruction. Every child is intrinsically curious: children desire knowledge, boundaries, and affirmation. You will not be able to reach each child in the same way, so diversity is the key. Use variety in your classroom and watch the fruits of your labor flourish into an awesome phenomenon for every child in your class.

We used to educate our children on how to act in school; I'm finding that this is no longer the case. Each day, we see the critical lack of parental teaching with which our children come to us, and we use these realities as the excuse for not educating students on how to conduct themselves, how to study at home, and how to become a responsible person. Educating your student is equivalent to training them on a larger scale. You cannot expect them to give you certain behaviors, responses, and competencies if you have not given them the proper data and information from which they can draw. You cannot expect them to read your mind and model the behaviors, actions, and responses you want. You cannot punish them for not being perfect, but you cannot lower your expectations.

Train, train, train!

Reflections

What are your feelings about a child's ability to learn?

_____

_____

_____

What grade, subjects, and methods of instruction are most comfortable for you?

_____

_____

_____

What areas in the realm of educating will you have to work on (for example, small group instruction, assertive discipline, etc.)?

_____

_____

_____

Tips to Help You Educate Everybody

- Read the books on the suggested readings list at the end of this book.

- Be sure to acquire materials for your classroom that are at or above your grade level.

- Use small groups often.

- Allow opportunities for students to talk about the lessons.

- Grade assignments daily: this is a compass to guide instruction.

- Communicate often with parents regarding students' learning. Do it through phone calls, e-mail, text messaging, etc.

Service

Definition:

1. an act of helpful activity; help, aid
2. the supplying or supplier of utilities or commodities, as water, electricity, or gas, required or demanded by the public.
3. the providing or a provider of accommodation and activities required by the public, as maintenance, repair
4. something made or done by a commercial organization for the public benefit and without regard to direct profit

Synonyms:

account, advantage, applicability, appropriateness, assistance, avail, benefit, business, courtesy, dispensation, duty, employment, labor, usefulness, value, work

Service Quotes:

The true leader serves. Serves people. Serves their best interests, and in doing so will not always be popular, may not always impress. But because true leaders are motivated more by loving concern than a desire for personal glory, they are willing to pay the price.
Eugene Habecker

I don't know what your destiny will be, but one thing I know: the ones among you who will be really happy are those who have sought and found how to serve.

Albert Schweitzer

The things I do for you are not necessarily meant to be repaid, but I do them because you need me and because I care.

SRJ

S is for Service

Building a wholesome classroom begins with an attitude that is committed to service. Seeing the classroom with the eyes of a servant is one of the keys to longevity in this profession. You must see yourself as an agent of goodwill. You must realize from the onset that you are now a professional helper who reports for duty five days a week, under conditions that may be a bit less than ideal. This realization is vital, because all too often you don't get what you deserve in a paycheck. Many times teachers have to take a part-time job to help pay for the extras in life. As teachers, we are not always shown the appreciation and recognition to which we are truly entitled. Often a teacher will have to function outside the state's issued job description and act as a nurse, hair stylist, seamstress, nutritionist, absentee parent, crossing guard, preacher, club sponsor, after-hours day care worker, children's advocate, parent's advocate, policeman, and the list goes on. Own the attitude that embraces service and you will find total peace in your career. The classroom is not the place for selfishness or selfish people.

Reflections

If there were one thing that you could change about the teaching profession, what would it be and why?

_____

_____

_____

Why did you choose this profession?

_____

_____

_____

Tips for Staying Service-Oriented at Work

- ♥ Remind yourself that you are an agent of goodwill.
- ♥ You will not always receive the proper credit for what you do—let it go!
- ♥ Never go to work angry.
- ♥ Stop complaining.
- ♥ Pray.
- ♥ Meditate.
- ♥ Laugh!

Order

Definition:

1. an authoritative direction or instruction; command; mandate
2. the disposition of things following one after another, as in space or time; succession or sequence
3. a condition in which each thing is properly disposed with reference to other things and to its purpose; methodical or harmonious arrangement
4. customary mode of procedure; established practice or usage
5. conformity or obedience to law or established authority
6. state or condition generally
7. proper, satisfactory, or working condition
8. prevailing course or arrangement of things; established system or regime

Synonyms:

classification, sequence, pattern, plan, system, condition, layout, formation, distribution, disposal, lineup, management, establishment, grouping

Order Quotes:

Art . . . is an attempt to bring order out of chaos.

Stephen Sondheim

Good order is the foundation of all great things.

Edmund Burke

Order and simplification are the first steps toward the mastery of a subject.

Thomas Mann

Civilization begins with order, grows with liberty, and dies with chaos.

Will Durant

Respectful and/or responsible procedures to ensure productivity.

SRJ

O is for Order

Wholesome classrooms exhibit order in these areas: classroom management, clerical reports, general paperwork, and learning environment. Wholesome classrooms have a definite sense of mutual respect. There are systemic routines and rituals that are built into each day so that each day runs effectively and smoothly. A classroom schedule sequences components that maximize learning. Paperwork and records must be in order, so devise a system quickly, even if you must ask for help. A paper trail is a good way to keep up with work, but technology-based recording is even better. Get "plugged-in," don't shy away from advances in technology.

Lesson plans order the scope and sequence of your state's standards, so make sure your plans are doable. Planning and implementation require order because educating children is not a haphazard occurrence. The presentation of the classroom should depict order, especially as it relates to function and age-appropriate embellishments. Order can even minimize disruptive behavior. Failure to keep order in your classroom can jeopardize your overall academic delivery.

Also, keep order in your personal life. Many times our personal lives overflow into our work and affect our performance by making us cranky, tired, and unpleasant. Teachers have the tendency to take themselves for granted and this puts us at risk for bad health. Drink lots of liquids and get plenty of rest. Stop taking the laptop to bed with you, especially if you are married. Take a weekend excursion from time to time. Work out, try yoga, or treat yourself to a bubble bath.

Recently, after being diagnosed with lupus, I decided to start taking care of myself. Getting my life in order meant taking a break from worrying and from taking care of the world—I started taking care of myself. Although I often go to church, my position and responsibilities there would sometimes feel like a second job. I had no outlet. I started taking care of myself by redecorating my bedroom and actually creating a sanctuary, with rich colors and candles. This was the first time I had really focused on making me happy on such a grand scale. I would just be there for hours, without a sound. Sometimes I would watch my favorite "make me happy" movie, *What About Bob?* starring Bill Murray and Richard Dreyfuss, and get my laugh on! Over time, I started to take small "Me-Time Dates" and vacations. The reality is that many of the illnesses we suffer from are the results of stress due to the lack of order in our lives. We have to come to a point when we stop blaming others and chaotic situations and take a real look at ourselves. The body can only take so much abuse, be it intentional or unintentional. Your mind can only take so much stress. Therefore, teachers must take time to replenish themselves. No, we may never have a school workshop geared towards rest and renewal. Sometimes, however, we do get an occasional pep talk at Institute, which must carry us for the whole school year. Simply put, if you do not take care of yourself, then you will have nothing to give to others.

Reflections

What comes to mind when you think about order in the classroom?

_____

_____

_____

What is your responsibility when it comes to order in your classroom?

_____

_____

_____

How can you order your personal life so that your work life is more productive?

_____

_____

_____

Tips for Acquiring and Maintaining Order in the Classroom

- Devise arrival and dismissal procedures for your classroom.
- Utilize a sign-in and sign-out procedure that's age-appropriate for your class.
- Assign jobs and responsibilities to your students that will make transitions run smoothly in the classroom.
- Provide a homework center or central location.
- Communicate with parents in writing or by phone on a weekly or daily basis.
- Pay close attention to daily, weekly, and monthly office reports, and submit them as required.
- Take care of yourself and schedule "Me-Time Dates."

Mentor

Definition:

1. A wise and trusted counselor or teacher
2. To serve as a trusted counselor or teacher, especially in occupational settings
3. To serve as a trusted counselor or teacher to (another person).

Synonyms:

advisor, counselor, guide, tutor, teacher, guru

Mentor Quotes:

Mentor: someone whose hindsight can become your foresight.

Anonymous

Mentoring is a brain to pick, an ear to listen, and a push in the right direction.

John Crosby

If you would thoroughly know anything, teach it to others.

Tryon Edwards

He is forced to be literate about the illiterate, witty about the witless, and coherent about the incoherent.

Anonymous

Passing the torch and fostering a legacy.

SRJ

M is for Mentoring

Building a wholesome classroom isn't an automatic gift, but a purpose driven act. Getting everything to click and make sense at first may be a bit hard and burdensome, but just hang in there. Building a wholesome classroom can be a learned skill. Young teachers must humble themselves—despite their eagerness—and give of themselves to be mentored. Experienced teachers must be willing to mentor new teachers. Proper mentoring can sharpen both individuals and benefit student success at the same time. Mentoring can eliminate some of the unnecessary trials and errors that come with the occupation. If you are not assigned a mentor by your administrator at the beginning of your teaching career, then find your own. Look around and seek out the most innovative, positive person around and just ask them to mentor you. Most teachers will not turn you down.

I remember early on in my career, a young lady—who is now a principal—came up to me in a workshop. Our principal evidently had told her that I would be at the workshop and to introduce herself to me. Well, this young lady said to me, "I'm going to hold on to you because I want what you have." I was speechless, but I said OK. That made me realize the seriousness of my job: I had to be an example and a coach. I'm so very proud of her today and often communicate with her whenever the need arises. I have served as a student-teacher supervisor as well as a reading coach, and I consider that level of service an honor.

We have to be willing to help someone else by mentoring.

Reflections

What are your feelings about mentoring in the field of education?

_____

_____

_____

In what areas can you benefit from mentoring and being mentored?

_____

_____

_____

Tips to Help You Benefit from the Mentoring Process

- Be open.
- Don't take constructive suggestions personally (I cried the first time!).
- Choose a mentor who still enjoys teaching.
- Don't worry if things don't work out at first.
- Do your *best*, but always strive for *great*!

Tips for Being a Better Mentor

- Be open.
- Show you care.
- Be patient.
- Share your failures as well as your successes.
- Meet consistently.
- Share latest strategies and model instruction when

necessary.

Enjoy

Definition:

1. To take pleasure or satisfaction in the possession or experience
2. to be delighted with
3. to have, possess, and use with satisfaction
4. to occupy or have the benefit of, as a good and profitable thing

Synonyms:

delight, pleasure, good, well-liked, desirable, satisfy

Enjoy Quotes:

A contented mind is the greatest blessing a man can enjoy in this world.
Joseph Addison

I want ordinary people to enjoy a decent standard of living, with ever increasing security, comfort, and joy.
Gloria Macapagal-Arroyo

Life's little rewards that come along with endurance and perseverance.
SRJ

E is for Enjoy

Enjoy each new day as it presents itself. There is never a dull moment in a classroom. Children come packed with anecdotes and surprises that will be with you for a lifetime. You will learn some of your greatest life lessons from your classroom experiences. Children almost always remember their teachers, especially those who impact their lives the most. Although our job is complex, teaching is still one of the most rewarding careers around. Enjoy your job! Do whatever it takes to keep your classroom beautiful. Have fun with your students! We have to work at relationships, and that includes in the classroom, too. If you are not happy with the classroom environment that you have created, then try something else.

Keep your classroom alive and fresh. Play music, include

more crafts, and keep a pleasant fragrance. Bring in a few furnishings from home, or try a pet or two. Incorporate puzzles, guest readers, and snack days into your workweek. Try having class outside or challenging other classes. Schedule extra field trips aside from those already on the roster and incorporate Internet learning extensions. Change can be good!

If you aren't willing to go the extra mile, then maybe you need to try something else. Failing to enjoy your job creates decay in your career.

New teachers must realize that how you start off in this career is a pretty good indicator of how you will end up. Administrators are looking for fresh people who enjoy what they do and who are willing to go the extra mile. Actually, this profession is the very vehicle through which all other careers are derived.

The school is one of America's most enduring institutions, the foundation that helps shape the nation and establishes individual lives. Restoring wholesome functions in education will greatly reshape the world. As teachers, we educate the masses, build legacies, and jump-start destinies. Wholesome classrooms begin with wholesome teachers. Wholesome teachers are vital to building wholesome citizens. So enjoy life and enjoy impacting America for the good of us all!

Reflections

What did you enjoy most about your school days?

_____

_____

_____

What are your plans to help make your students' school days with you special?

_____

_____

_____

Tips to Help You Enjoy Your Career

- ♥ Share your story with your students.
- ♥ Incorporate music and art often.
- ♥ Invite guest presenters to your class.
- ♥ Celebrate class benchmarks.
- ♥ Take field trips that are different and fun.
- ♥ Conduct class outside.
- ♥ Acknowledge birthdays in a creative way.
- ♥ Read funny stories to your class.
- ♥ Laugh!

Wholesome Classrooms Foster a Sense of Community in your Classroom

Like most things in education, these ideas are not new; they are practices that teachers have used over time and that I can personally attest to that work.

1. Use the computer to create attractive personalized name tags at the beginning of the school year.

2. Send flyers or mail postcards before the school year begins to welcome students to their new classroom.

3. As an alternative to class names that are animal-related, try a class name that students can grow into, thereby benefiting from the self-fulfilling prophecy: for example, Johnson's Jewels, or William's Whiz Kids.

4. Get a classroom mother or father.

5. Do a monthly or quarterly newsletter that includes homework tips, reminders, birthdays, student of the month, honor roll, etc.

6. Create a book about you: include pictures of your family and past students. Share it during a "Read Aloud," especially at the beginning of the school year.

7. Always start the year with a social studies unit, such as "All About Me," or "I'm Me, I'm Special."(Include Read

Alouds that include school themes, diversity, ethics, and individuality themes.) This is a smart way to teach desired behaviors and create a sense of belonging in your class.

8. Send nice notes home with children often.

9. Do class affirmations often.

10. Give frequent praise.

11. Send students a message that they're important: greet each morning with a smile.

12. Celebrate birthdays and academic milestones.

13. Join your school's PTA.

14. Post class work often.

15. Encourage journal writing and allow your students to see you writing at the assigned time as well. This is also a great management skill to use after P.E., lunch, assemblies, etc.

16. Have a sustained silent reading time (10 minutes) and allow your students to see you reading at this assigned time as well. This is also a great management skill to use after P.E., lunch, assemblies, etc.

17. Orient students to the school and the faculty at the onset of the school year.

Parent and Faculty Emergency Phone List (you can never have this information in too many places!)

My "TO DO" List For the First Few Days of School

_____

_____

_____

_____

_____

_____

_____

_____

_____

_____

_____

_____

Journal Writing

Reflections from the first 21 days of school: it has been said that it takes 21 days to make or break a habit. Take note of your first 21 days and learn from them.

Date _____

_____

_____

_____

_____

Date _____

_____

_____

_____

_____

Date _____

_____
_____
_____
_____

Date _____

_____
_____
_____
_____

Date _____

_____
_____
_____
_____

Date _____

_____
_____
_____
_____

Date _____

_____
_____
_____
_____

Date _____

_____
_____
_____
_____

Date _____

_____
_____
_____
_____

Date _____

_____
_____
_____
_____

Date _____

_____
_____
_____
_____

Date _____

_____
_____
_____
_____

Date _____

_____
_____
_____
_____

Date _____

_____
_____
_____
_____
_____

Date _____

_____
_____
_____
_____

Date _____

_____
_____
_____
_____

Date _____

_____
_____
_____
_____

Date _____

_____

_____

_____

_____

Date _____

_____

_____

_____

_____

Date _____

_____

_____

_____

_____

_____

Date _____

Suggested Readings

The First Few Days of School by Harry K. Wong and Rosemary T. Wong

Assertive Discipline by Lee Canter

Strategies That Work by Stephanie Harvey and Anne Goudvis

Apprenticeship in Literacy by Linda Dorn, Cathy French and Tammy Jones

Comprehension: Strategic Instruction for K-3 Students by Grethen Owock

On Solid Ground-Strategies for Teaching Reading K-3 by Sharon Taberski

Reading with Meaning by Debbie Miller

Spaces and Places by Debbie Diller

Acknowledgments

It *does* take a village of wholesome people to raise one child—thank you!

To My Family:

My mother, Stella Johnson
My grandfather and grandmother, Alfred and Mary Hughes
My father and stepmother, Eddie and Patricia Johnson
My daughter, Ayanna Johnson
My siblings: Eddie Jr, Regina, and Joyce

To My Extended Family:

Dr. Derrick E. Houston, Sr.
Warriors International Fellowship Church Family
The Faculty and Staff of Robinson Elementary, Fairfield, Alabama (past and present)
AMRAE Publishing Group and Mr. Marc Raby

To My Village:

Birmingham Public Schools
Lawson State Community College

Miles College
Robinson Elementary, Fairfield, Alabama
Fairfield City Schools

Alabama Reading Initiative
Pastor Timothy Woods, Hopewell Church Family
Mrs. Deborah Chiles
Strayer University and Dr. Karen Day
Dr. Sharon Bell, Birmingham Public Schools

About the Author

Sonya R. Johnson is a parent, an educator, a motivational speaker, and an elder in her church. As a teacher for over 17 years and presently a reading coach in the Fairfield City school system, she has mentored and supervised a vast number of college students and new teachers. She addresses critical issues affecting children's social and cognitive development. The central theme of her message empowers new teachers to take care of themselves early on, to become effective leaders, and to maximize their individual potential in the classroom. She also encourages experienced teachers to continue in their calling with zeal and compassion. She is currently studying for master degrees in Education and in Christian Counseling. She is a graduate of the historic and prestigious Miles

College in Fairfield, Alabama.

Wholesome Classrooms is a movement to encourage teachers to build a wholesome classroom environment. In this handbook you will find a time-tested, teacher-recommended compilation of ingredients that can help take the mystery out of successful longevity in the educational profession. In this guide, you'll explore must-have attributes for career success and thought-provoking questions for reflection and life application in the classroom. Designed for individual, whole group, or small group study, this guide helps you to:

- ♥ Remember fundamental attributes and principles that will ground you in the classroom.
- ♥ Explore varied perspectives of the most important characteristics and practices that are vital for the development of the whole child.
- ♥ Enrich your understanding of the importance of maturity in the classroom.

Apply key suggestions and tips to real-life circumstances.

Fulfill your true purpose and potential in life as a great teacher, administrator, or youth leader.

Great For:

                        College Classes

                        Staff Development

                        Professional Book Study

                        New Teacher Academy

                        Student Teachers

                        PTA/PTO Discussions

                        Mega Conferences

. . . . and many more

www.ingramcontent.com/pod-product-compliance
Lightning Source LLC
LaVergne TN
LVHW051509070426
835507LV00022B/3001